ALSO BY JEFF FOXWORTHY

*You Might Be a Redneck If . . . This Is the
Biggest Book You've Ever Read*

There's No Place Like a Mobile Home for the Holidays

*The Redneck Grill: The Most Fun You Can Have with
Fire, Charcoal, and a Dead Animal*

Redneck Extreme Mobile Home Makeover

Jeff Foxworthy's

REDNECK
DICTIONARY

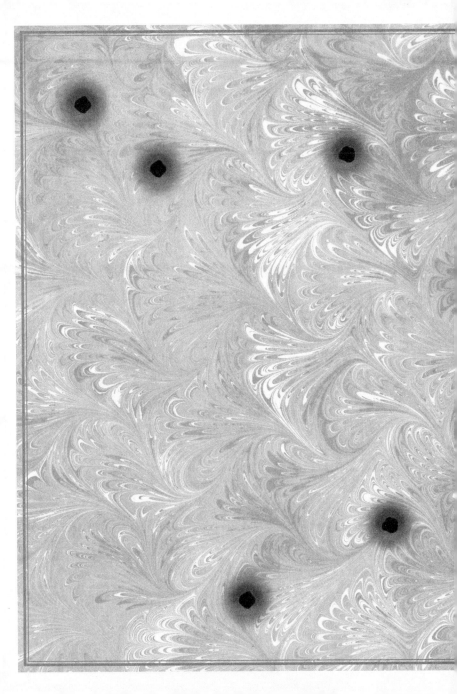

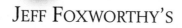

JEFF FOXWORTHY'S

REDNECK DICTIONARY

*Words You Thought You
Knew the Meaning Of*

JEFF FOXWORTHY

with FAX BAHR, ADAM SMALL,
GARY CAMPBELL, *and* BRIAN HARTT

Illustrations by LAYRON DE JARNETTE

VILLARD NEW YORK

Published in the United States by Villard Books,
an imprint of The Random House Publishing Group,
a division of Random House, Inc., New York.

VILLARD and "V" CIRCLED Design are registered trademarks
of Random House, Inc.

ISBN 1-4000-6465-1

Printed in the United States of America on acid-free paper

www.villard.com

19 18 17 16 15 14 13

Book design by Susan Turner

PREFACE

Redneck words. The idea originally began early in my career when people in New York, L.A., and Chicago made fun of the words I used in everyday conversation. Like "Did you eat yet?" was really just one word: *Jeet-yet?*

As the idea expanded, I realized there were actual real words that me and my family and friends used in a totally different way than Webster intended. Like *mayonnaise* used in a sentence was "Mayonnaise a lot of people here tonight." *European* became "Hey dude, turn that way! European on my boot!"

When we began *Blue Collar TV* we featured some of these words as short skits. They quickly became an audience favorite.

Well, there's plenty more where they came from. Here's several hundred to make you think, to make you laugh, and to make you one of the goodest talkers of the English language. If you still don't understand it after reading this book, stalk about it over a cup of coffee.

Keep laughing,
Jeff Foxworthy

JEFF FOXWORTHY'S

REDNECK
DICTIONARY

ALLOWED

afar (ə-fär´), *n.* an object in the state of combustion. *"There's no sense bein' this cold—let's build afar."*

Alas·ka (əl-ask´-ə), *n. and v.* to resolve to make an inquiry. *"If I wanna know where to find a polar bear, Alaska guy who lives here."*

al·lowed (ə-laủd´), *adj.* distinguished by an intense elevation of volume. *"Did you just hear allowed noise?"*

an·nu·ity (ə-nü´-ət-ē), *n. and v.* having fore-thought or intuition. *"I couldn't hear him, but annuity was sayin'."*

ap·par·ent (ə-per´-ənt), *n.* one who sires or gives birth to offspring. *"It's obvious to me from lookin' at yer belly that yer gonna be **apparent**."*

Ar·ma·ged·don (ärm-ə-ge´-din), *n. and v.* putting oneself in a position for action. *"I tell ya, if it gets any crazier, **Armageddon** outta here."*

ar·ma·ture (är´-mə-chŭr), *v. and adj.* displaying exceptional wisdom, experience, and/or age. *"I know sometimes I acts like a kid but I really **armature**."*

as·i·nine (as´-ə-nīn), *n.* favorable praise of the hind end, to the positive ninth integer. *"Man, I would give her face a two and her **asinine**."*

ARMAGEDDON

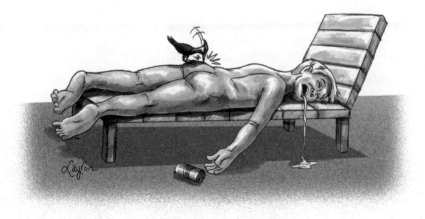

ASPECT

as·par·a·gus (ə-sperˊ-ə-gəs), *n.* ambivalence about having to install a replacement for an air-filled rubber wheel. *"I got a flat, so I'm gonna have to put on **asparagus**."*

as·pect (asˊ-pekt), *n. and v.* having one's backside assaulted by a sharp object. *"He got done skinny-dippin', passed out on that deck chair, and had his **aspect** by a woodpecker."*

asth·ma (azˊ-mə), *v.* to make an inquiry to a person of familiar acquaintance. *"I don't know if I can go or not. Lemme **asthma** wife."*

at·om (atˊ-əm), *prep. and n.* in the direction of something or someone. *"Two deer jumped outta the woods and we just started shootin' **atom**."*

at·tacks (ə-taks´), *n.* a percentage of one's assets taken annually by a governing body. *"If you let 'em, I swear the government would put **attacks** on the air."*

av·e·nue (av´-ə-nü), *n. and v.* to declare possession of something recently acquired. *"**Avenue** address, but I don't remember it."*

ban·ner (ban´-ər), *v. and n.* to prohibit a female person from a specific location. *"Cody's grandma cusses so much, they're gonna **banner** from the Little League park."*

bar·ri·er (ber´-ē-ər), *v. and n.* to conceal or cover a female, usually under earth or debris. *"She died while on vacation, so I think they decided to **barrier** on the beach."*

BARRIER

BELIEVE

bay·ou (bī´-ü), *v. and n.* to purchase for another. *"I just walked right up to her and said, 'Hey darlin', lemme bayou a drink.'* "

beer (bir´), *v.* to express one's desire to remain at a specific location, usually during intoxication. *"I'll beer till ten, then I gotta get home."*

bee·tle (bē´-təl), *v. and conj.* to exist for an unspecified amount of time. *"How long do you think it's gonna beetle they figure out we're gone?"*

be·lieve (bē-lēv´), *n. and v.* a demand for the *Bombus ruderatus* to vacate the immediate vicinity. *"Oh no! I'm allergic! Believe me alone!"*

be·moan (bē-mōn´), *v. and adj.* to declare posses-sion by oneself. *"I don't like takin' orders. That's why I gotta **bemoan** boss."*

big·ots (big´-əts), *adj.* used to describe a large ob-ject in motion or action. *"Man, Al's belly is so **bigots** draggin' on the floor."*

bit·ter (bit´-ər), *v. and n.* involving the closing of jaws, as done on a female. *"She kept teasin' that dog till he finally **bitter**."*

bob·ble (bäb´-əl), *n. and v.* the confident predic-tion for future action, to be effected by a person named Robert. *"Don't worry, Marge. **Bobble** get us out of here."*

BOBBLE

BOMBARDIER

bob·sled (bäbs´-led), *n. and v.* the act of guidance by a person named Robert. *"I ain't no expert, but I think **bobsled** us down the wrong path."*

bom·bar·dier (bamb´-ə-dir), *v. and n.* to attack an *Odocoileus virginianus* with an explosive device. *"When I'm huntin' I usually use my rifle, but sometimes I just take out dynamite and **bombardier**."*

bro·ker (brōk´-ər), *v. and adj.* to have violently injured any thing or things belonging to a female. *"My mom fell off a ladder and **broker** arm."*

bud·get (bəj´-ət), *v. and n.* to transfer an object from one location to another. *"Papaw was workin' on my car and it fell on his foot. I tried to pull it off, but I couldn't **budget**!"*

bur·den (bərd´-in), *n. and prep.* indicating the specific location of a flying creature. *"A **burden** the hand is worth two in the bush."*

but·ter·fly (bət-ər-flī´), *conj. and n.* an exception concerning the opening in pants worn by a female. *"I didn't mean to embarrass her, **butterfly** was open!"*

cab·i·net (kab´-ən-it), *n.* used in reference to an event taking place within a vehicle employed for ferrying passengers. *"When we were in New York, we got in a **cabinet** stunk!"*

Cal·cut·ta (kal-kət´-ə), *n. and v. (usu. vulgar)* the release of intestinal gas by a person named Calvin. *"Well, far as I can tell, **Calcutta** fart and then somebody struck a match."*

CALCUTTA

CANTALOUPE

can·dy (kand´-ē), *v. and n.* negative verb for a male unable to act. *"Why **candy** just ask you one simple question?"*

can·o·py (kan-ə-pē´), *n.* a metal vessel used for the containment of urine. *"The dude never stops for bathroom breaks. That's why there's a **canopy** in his truck."*

can·ta·loupe (kant´-ə-lōp), *v.* the expressed inability to marry in secret. *"My daddy wants a traditional marriage, honey, so I **cantaloupe**."*

can·ti·le·ver (kant´-ə-lēv-ər), *v. and n.* to inquire about the possibilities for ending a relationship. *"The preacher said till death do us part, but **cantilever** if she fools around on me?"*

cap·i·tal (kap´-ət-il), *n. and v.* regarding an action concerning the future of any covering used to close off a receptacle. *"Careful with that bottle—if you don't put on that **capital** spill."*

car·go (kär´-gō), *n. and v.* an automobile moving on a certain course, usually forward. *"Can't you make this **cargo** any faster?"*

cash·ier (kash´-ir), *n.* any medium for fiscal exchange, in a specific place. *"I tried to pay by check, but the lady behind the register told me they only take **cashier**."*

ca·si·no (kəs-ē´-nō), *conj. and v.* a phrase concerning a gentleman with particular knowledge. *"When I go to Vegas, I go with my buddy Roy, **casino** more about gamblin' than I do."*

CARGO

CHAPTER

cas·trate (kast´-rāt), *n.* a hardened plaster mold used for immobilizing a broken limb so that the bone will not heal crookedly. *"They're gonna have to rebreak my arm 'cause they said the doctor didn't get the **castrate** the first time."*

cat·e·go·ry (kat´-ə-gȯr-ē), *n. and adj.* a domesticated feline bleeding profusely from excessive trauma. *"That guy hit Fluffy goin' fifty miles an hour and left that **category** mess."*

cen·sure (sent´-shər), *conj. and v.* pertaining to an ongoing condition of the person addressed. *"I'll have another drink, **censure** payin'."*

chap·ter (chapt´-ər), *v. and adj.* to have received epidermal roughening. *"That wind **chapter** lips up pretty good."*

•

chauf·feur (shō´-fər), *n. and prep.* a reference to a performance. *"There's nekkid girls inside, boys, and I can get you into the chauffeur just two dollars!"*

clas·si·fied (klas´-əf-īd), *n. and conj.* pertaining to regret over a course at school. *"I'd have gone to classified been smarter."*

cof·fee (kȯf´-ē), *v. and n.* to explosively expel air from the lungs, as performed by a male. *"My granddad's got a cold, and every time he tries to coffee wets his pants."*

col·umn (käl´-əm), *v. and n.* an imperative regarding electronic communication with a specific male. *"Daddy likes you best, dude, so you column."*

COLUMN

CONDOM

co·ma (kōm´-ə), *v.* to groom hair using a multi-toothed tool. *"When you're a barber you have to **coma** lot of ugly heads."*

con·dom (känd´-əm), *v. and n.* having purpose-fully swindled a gullible male for personal gain. *"She **condom** into thinkin' she was on the pill."*

con·vey·or (kən-va´-ər), *v. and adj.* to transmit a nonpresent female's communications. *"My wife couldn't be here, but she wanted me to **conveyor** sympathies."*

cous·in (kəz´-ən), *conj.* for a reason, specifically re-lating to a particular place. *"You can't sleep with your relatives, **cousin** the big city that's a crime."*

cus·tom (kəst´-əm), *v. and n.* to have voiced vulgar language at a person or persons. *"When them Jehovah's Witnesses came to our house, Granddaddy done **custom** out."*

cut·ter (kət´-ər), *v. and adj.* to use a sharp instrument to separate one thing from another, as performed by a female. *"If Sheila don't **cutter** toenails soon, I'm filin' for a divorce."*

de·bate (də-bāt´), *n.* anything used to entice prey. *"I don't wanna argue no more 'bout which worm we're gonna use for **debate**."*

de·fense (di-fents´), *n.* a barrier bisecting a piece of land. *"I told him to drive through da gate and the damn dummy drove through **defense**."*

CUTTER

DEFINITE

def·i·nite (def´-ən-it), *adj. and n.* of or pertaining to a person who is hearing impaired. *"My grandma's real **definite** affects the odds on her life expectancy."*

de·lights (di-līts´), *n.* electrical devices used for illumination. *"Hey, stupid, turn out **delights**."*

de·mo·graph·ic (dem-ə-gra´-fik), *n. and adj.* referring to visually explicit material. *"**Demographic** photos in that dirty magazine."*

den·i·grate (den´-i-grāt), *adv. and adj.* a reference to the ensuing occurrence of something large and/or wondrous. *"First my stomach hurt, and **denigrate** wind came outta my rear end, and now I feel a whole lot better."*

den·tal (dent´-əl), *n. and v.* to do with the result of a crease or a depression in all types of metal plating. *"Well, the good news is that little **dental** come out real easy."*

de·scent (di-sent´), *n.* an olfactory emission. *"The dogs lost **descent** right about here."*

de·tail (di-tāl´), *n.* an appendage extending from the buttocks, usually covered with hair. *"Best way to catch a skunk is just to grab him by **detail**."*

de·void (di-vȯid´), *n.* an absence of matter. *"**Devoid** that woman left in my heart is as big as a truck."*

DESCENT

DIRECTION

di·et (dī´-ət), *v. and n.* to change the hue of something. *"You know what you oughta do with your hair, Barb, is **diet** red."*

di·gest (dī´-jest), *v. and adv.* to expire, especially recently. *"I don't know why Daddy had to **digest** three days after Mama."*

di·men·sion (də-men´-shən), *n.* an instance of casually calling attention to something. *"Just **dimension** of pork and beans makes me gassy."*

di·rec·tion (də-rek´-shən), *n.* the engorgement of the male sex organ. *"Doc, could you give my Hank here a sample of those little blue pills? **Direction** ain't what it used to be."*

dis·co (dis´-kō), *n. and v.* referring to the intended or proper location of a specific thing; usually used with an inquiry. *Query in operating room: "I put everything else back . . . but now where's **disco**?"*

dis·gust·ed (di-skəst´-id), *v. and n.* to have verbally considered or examined a specific subject. *"Billy, your mother and I have **disgusted**, and we both think you're on steroids."*

dis·may (dis-mā´), *n. and v.* something raised as a possibility. *"**Dismay** come as a surprise, ma'am, but you're not pregnant."*

dis·tress (dis-tres´), *n.* a skirted garment, especially of a full-figured person. *"Does **distress** make my butt look fat?"*

DISCO

DOMAIN

di·verse (də-vərs´), *n.* a lyrical, nonrepeating stanza within a song. *"I've got the chorus, but **diverse** is still givin' me trouble."*

doc·tor (däkt´-ər), *v. and adj.* to have applied to a female employee a punitive measure in which a percentage of her wages are garnisheed. *"After my wife wrecked that forklift, they **doctor** pay for the next six months."*

do·main (dō-mān´), *v.* to lack importance. *"Don't let it bug you, man. It **domain** a thing."*

dou·bloon (də-bloon´), *n.* any single object having a hue in the color spectrum between green and violet. *"You can wear the brown hat or the green hat, but don't touch **doubloon**."*

drag·on (dra´-gən), *v.* being brought into, usually by force. *"Don't be **dragon** me into your argument."*

Ee

ear (ir´), *v.* to receive and cognitively process sound. *"Huh? I couldn't **ear** a single word you said."*

elix·ir (i-liks´-ər), *n. and v.* the act, by a male mammal, of lapping any specific female with his tongue. *"My dog wakes my daughter up every mornin'. He jumps on the bed and **elixir** face."*

em·bark (im-bärk´), *n. and v.* referring to the production of the short, sharp cry characteristic of the male of the species *Canis familiaris*. *"That dog's so well behaved you can't make **embark**."*

ELIXIR

EMIGRATE

em·i·grate (em-ə-grāt´), *n. and adj.* an egotistical inquiry. *"I nailed us some pretty good seats here, dude. **Emigrate** or what?"*

emo·tions (i-mō´-shəns), *n. and v.* to indicate something with gestures, as performed by a male. *"Every time he makes a big play, **emotions** to the crowd to make more noise."*

en·close (in-klōz´), *n.* attired in garments. *"She looks good **enclose**, but she looks better out of them."*

en·coun·ter (in-kaún´-tər), *v.* to respond to one offer with another. *"Find out what he's askin' for it **encounter** with a lower offer."*

en·e·ma (en´-ə-mə), *n. and v.* declaring one's state of being or whereabouts. *"Dang it all! My car broke down, **enema** good ten miles from a gas station."*

en·roll (in-rōl´), *conj. and v.* to move by revolving or turning over repeatedly. *"I told you, Lloyd, if you catch on fire you're supposed to stop, drop, **enroll**."*

eras·es (i-rā´-səz), *n. and v.* competing in a contest involving speed, especially by any person named Dale Jr. *"Dale Jr. is the man. **Erases** anybody, anywhere."*

es·ca·la·tor (esk´-ə-lā-tər), *v.* to make a planned or scheduled inquiry. *"I got a question, but I'm kinda busy right now, so could I **escalator**?"*

ENROLL

EUPHRATES

es·cape (is-kāp´), *n.* a long, hanging garment worn on a man's back. *"I wouldn't have known he was a superhero, but **escape** gave him away."*

Eu·phra·tes (yŭ-frāt´-ēz), *n. and adj.* to be in fear of bodily harm from a male. *"What's the matter, Timmy? **Euphrates** gonna hit ya?"*

ex·pend (eks-spend´), *n. and v.* one's former spouse on a buying spree. *"Dang! You should see my **expend** money."*

eye·lash (ī-lash´), *n. and v.* acting with aggression toward another. *"I feel bad when **eyelash** out at my wife."*

fe·ces (fē´-sēz), *conj. and v.* a conditional expression involving concern about being witnessed or discovered, often involving an illicit activity. *"Feces us together, the you-know-what is gonna hit the fan."*

fe·tus (fēt´-əs), *v. and n.* to provide for group mastication. *"I wonder what they're gonna fetus for lunch."*

feud (fyüd´), *conj. and v.* involving any supposition concerning the action of another person. *"I woulda never shot at you, feud never shot at me."*

fid·dle (fid´-əl), *conj. and v.* regarding speculation on the result of an action about to be undertaken. *"I wonder fiddle get me all the way to the moon?"*

FIDDLE

FITNESS

fire (fi´-ər), *conj. and v.* an empathetic supposition involving placing oneself in another's position. *"Fire you, I'd look for a new place to live."*

fis·sion (fi´-shin), *n.* the act of capturing cold-blooded, aquatic craniate vertebrates. *"Ever since they put up that nuclear power plant, the fission been terrible."*

fit·ness (fit´-nəs), *v. and n.* to be able to wear a snug garment. *"And you didn't think I could fitness bathin' suit after three kids!"*

fix·ture (fiks´-chùr), *v.* to have repaired the property of another. *"It seems like you would be nicer to me since I just fixture car."*

fluo·res·cent (flȯr-es´-sint), *n. and v.* a negative declaration about the lowermost horizontal surface of a structure. *"You'd better mop it again, son. That fluorescent clean yet."*

fon·due (fän-dü´), *conj. and v.* involving uncertainty about a future action. *"I packed my own chute. I don't know fondue somethin' like that again."*

fore·close (fȯr-klōz´), *prep. and n.* pertaining to a wardrobe acquisition. *"Marla said she needed money foreclose. What the hell's wrong with the dress she's got?"*

for·eign (fȯr´-ən), *n. and prep.* anything done in an uninterrupted quadruplicate pattern. *"Them Montreal Canadiens are a good hockey team. They've won foreign a row."*

FONDUE

FREQUENT

fore·skin (fòrs´-kin), *n. and v.* the possibilities available to an unseen but powerful strength or energy. *"If you come to my side, Luke Skywalker, then the foreskin be with you."*

fo·rum (fòr´-əm), *prep. and n.* concerning alliance with others. *"The thing about NASCAR drivers is there's no gray area. You're either forum or against 'em."*

fräu·lein (fròil´-īn), *prep. and n.* a phrase used in declaring one's ignorance. *"Fräulein know, she ran away because of you."*

fre·quent (frēk´-wənt), *n. and v.* the path of any person afflicted with grotesque physical oddities. *"Oh yeah, Officer, the frequent most definitely thataway."*

fuel (fyül´), *conj. and v.* a conditional request of an individual concerning their future action. *"**Fuel** stay, I'll fix you another drink."*

ga·la (gal´-ə), *n. and v.* a woman inclined to take action. *"Her sister might be a dud, but that **gala** show you a good time!"*

ger·min·ate (jər´-mən-āt), *n. and v.* a person of Saxon ancestry who has completed mastication. *"I served Hansel a ninety-eight-ounce steak, and that there **germinate** the whole thing."*

ges·ture (jes´-chùr), *adv. and adj.* pertaining to a prediction of compatibility. *"He's **gesture** kinda guy."*

GESTURE

GROCER

glad·i·a·tor (glad´-ē-āt-ər), *adj. and v.* an exuberant reaction to the consumption of a female's cooking, by a male person. *"I'm **gladiator** muffins, or Grandma woulda been mad."*

god·dess (gäd´-əs), *n. and v.* the future action of a supreme being. *"**Goddess** gonna get you for that."*

gro·cer (grōs´-ər), *adj. and conj.* an inquiry regarding the extent of repulsiveness. *"Is he **grocer** what?"*

gui·tar (gət-tär´), *v. and n.* to perform an errand resulting in the acquisition of a bituminous liquid. *"If we're gonna fix this roof we're gonna have to **guitar**."*

har·dy (härd´-ē), *adv. and n.* a measure of force inflicted on a male. *"That boy got punched so **hardy** couldn't see straight."*

hay·wire (hā´-wī-ər), *interj. and v.* to question the motivation for a current action. *"**Haywire** you flirtin' with my wife?"*

heal (hēl´), *n. and v.* to predict or suppose the future action of a specific male. *"If that surgeon keeps drinkin', **heal** kill somebody."*

He·brews (hē´-brüz), *n. and v.* a statement concerning the ease with which a male will suffer a below-the-skin contusion. *"Don't be smackin' Timmy around like that, Cassie. **Hebrews** real easy."*

HARDY

HERESY

Hel·en (hel´-ən), *n. and conj.* the underworld, plus the aftermath. *"That poor guy's been to **Helen** back."*

he·lix (hē´-liks), *n. and v.* to drag the extended tongue along a person or object, as done by a male. *"It's below zero. If **helix** that fence his tongue is gonna get stuck."*

her·bi·cide (hər´-bə-sīd), *n. and adv.* a reference to the immediate surroundings of a woman. *"Sit **herbicide** the skinny guy so the boat don't tip over."*

her·e·sy (her´-ə-sē), *n. and v.* the visual perception of a mass of filamentous epidermal outgrowth. *"Y'all better get me some Rogaine, what with all the **heresy**."*

her·pes (hər´-pēz), *adj. and n.* small round vegetable seeds in the possession of a specific female. *"**Herpes** taste like they came out of a can."*

hip·pie (hip´-ē), *n.* a reference to the haunch of a specific male. *"Ever since he got shot in the **hippie** walks funny."*

hoard (hȯrd´), *v.* having committed an act of marital indiscretion, sometimes preceded by a financial interaction. *"She **hoard** around on him one too many times."*

Hol·land (häl´-ənd), *n. and conj.* half of a fairly popular pop duo from the late twentieth century. *"My favorite band is definitely **Holland** Oates."*

HIPPIE

HORRENDOUS

ho·ly (hōl´-ē), *n.* an indentation in the ground created by a specific male. *"That **holy** dug was deep."*

ho·ri·zon (hər-īz´-on), *n. and prep.* indicating a woman's focus on an object or her fervent desire, usually for something expensive. *"She's got **horizon** that mink coat."*

hor·ren·dous (hər-end´-əs), *n. and v.* any declaration concerning the backside of a female. *"She's got a pretty enough face, but **horrendous** huge and horrible."*

Il·li·nois (il´-ə-noi), *n. and v.* predicting bothersome or irritating behavior by a male. *"Jack's a pest. No matter what he says, **Illinois** ya."*

im·pa·tience (im-pā´-shənts), *n.* any group of impaired people confined to a place for healing. *"Impatience in the mental hospital scare me to death."*

In·dia (in´-dē-ə), *prep.* a function word indicating conditionality. *Flight attendant over the loudspeaker: "India 'vent of an emergency, your seat can be used as a toilet."*

in·her·it (in-her´-ət), *n.* concerning the interior location of the speaker. *"I don't know about outside, but inherit stinks."*

in·nu·en·do (in-yə-wen´-dō), *prep. and n.* indicating the passage of anything through a wall opening made of glass that can be opened or closed. *"Hey, dude, I just saw a bird fly innuendo."*

INNUENDO

INTENSE

in·qui·ries (in-kwīr´-ēz), *prep. and n.* referring to the actions of a specific male member of a vocal group. *"That boy's a monster at home, but **inquiries** a saint."*

in·tense (in-tents´), *prep. and n.* inside portable canvas shelters. *"Next time we go campin', I suggest we sleep **intense**."*

in·ter·cept (in-tər-sept´), *v. and conj.* concerning conditions placed on the permissibility of ingress. *"That there's the operatin' room. You can't **intercept** if you're a doctor."*

in·ter·face (in-tər-fās´), *prep. and n.* to a position of contact with the front part of a female's head. *"That guy hit a fastball and it flew right **interface**!"*

io·ta (ī-ōt´-ə), *n. and v.* first-person form of admitting debt. *"Sure I shot him, Officer, but in my defense, **iota** lotta money to that guy."*

iso·late (ī-sə-lāt´), *n. and v.* an explanation for extreme tardiness, usually in the form of an excuse. *"Sorry **isolate**, but I hit a deer on the way over here!"*

is·sue (ish-ü´), *n. and v.* concerning an ultimatum to another. *"Somebody's gotta go through that door first. Either **issue** or me, brother."*

Ja·kar·ta (jə-kär´-tə), *n. and prep.* pertaining to a person's automobile. *"Oh yeah, that mechanic at Tom's garage'll get **Jakarta** run real good."*

IOTA

JAMAICAN

Ja·mai·can (jə-māk´-ən), *n. and v.* an inquiry concerning another's creation. *"Hey there, Jimmy, what **Jamaican** for the science fair?"*

juic·i·er (joo´-sē-ər), *n. and v.* an inquiry concerning whether another has perceived, visually, a female; often involves the disrobed state of the subject. *"**Juicier** nekkid?"*

junc·ture (jənk´-chúr), *n. and adv.* a declaration of certainty pertaining to rubbish. *"You're throwin' it all out, but this **juncture** looks good to me."*

Ken·ya (ken´-yə), *v. and n.* to inquire as to the abilities of another. *"Hey, Rudy, **Kenya** hand me a beer?"*

kilt (kilt´), *v.* having caused a living thing to expire. *"If he was my husband, I'd have **kilt** him a long time ago."*

Ku·wait (kŭ-wāt´), *v.* indicating the ability to employ patience. *"I'm really hungry now, but I guess I **Kuwait**."*

lawn (lȯn´), *n.* a reference to the rules of a society; often used in connection with a popular television show. *"You catch that episode of **Lawn** Order last night?"*

let·ter car·ri·er (let´-ər-ka´-rē-ər), *v. and n.* to suggest that a woman transport her personal belongings herself. *"If she wants to bring all that junk, **letter carrier** own luggage."*

LETTER CARRIER

LICENSE

li·cense (lī-sints´), *n. and adv.* a reference to the most recent instance of fibbing. *"She ran over me with the pickup three days ago, and I ain't told a **license**."*

liv·er (liv´-ər), *v. and conj.* regarding options other than earthly existence. *"I'm so depressed I don't care if I **liver** die."*

man·da·rin (man´-də-rən), *interj. and n.* emphatically expressed concern about the state of two or more people. *"Lee and Bobby Chang just got back from Vegas, and **mandarin** a bad mood."*

man·i·fes·to (man-əf-əs´-tō), *interj. and n.* an expression of despair concerning a final chance, as for repair. *"**Manifesto** do it, I don't know what will."*

man·i·fold (man´-əf-ōld), *interj. and adj.* collo-
quial; expressing the possible future actions of an elderly person. "***Manifold** Mike hadn't a fallen into the
bear trap, he'd be with us today.*"

man·sion (man´-shən), *n. and v.* a phrase used to
warn about the negative repercussions of a male person's actions. "*That **mansion** be doin' that.*"

mar·ga·rine (märj´-ər-ən), *n. and v.* a reference to
the current location or situation of any woman named
Marge, along with her companion or companions.
"*Yup . . . Bob just took off, and I could be wrong, but I
think me and **margarine** big trouble.*"

mar·ma·lade (mär´-mə-lād), *n. and v.* a female
progenitor assuming a prone position. "*It was a sad
story. His **marmalade** down one day and just never got
up again.*"

MARGARINE

MASCOT

mar·shal (märsh´-əl), *n. and v.* a prediction concerning the future state of a wetland. *"That **marshal** swallow your tractor right up."*

mas·cot (mas´-kät), *n. and v.* indicating the condition or state of the Christian Eucharist. *"When old lady Watkins took a swing at the organist, I'd say that's right about when **mascot** out of hand."*

me·an·der (mē´-and-ər), *n.* a reference to one's self and a female. *"I would have gone out with Lucy, but **meander** cousin was already datin'."*

me·di·ate (mēd´-ē-ət), *n. and v.* animal flesh consumed by an individual male. *"No wonder his stomach burst, considerin' the amount of **mediate**."*

mis·trust (mis-trəst´), *n. and v.* an appeal to convince a female of one's honesty or reliability. *"**Mistrust** me on this one. I can fix your car."*

mo·dem (mōd´-əm), *v. and n.* to have cut or thrashed with a bladed machine. *"I thought about burnin' my front yard and my backyard, but I just **modem** instead."*

mol·li·fy (mäl´-əf-ī), *n. and conj.* concerning permission to proceed to a large indoor shopping complex, under certain promised conditions. *Teen girl on phone: "My mom says I can go to the **mollify** finish all my homework."*

mono·logue (män´-ə-lòg), *v. and n.* a declaration of one's position on a portion of cut timber. *"Please tell me I **monologue**."*

MONOLOGUE

MOTHER

mo·ron (mȯr´-än), *n. and prep.* the addition of a greater quantity to that already present. *"I told him that I already put hot sauce on the pizza, but the idiot just kept pourin' **moron**."*

mo·tel (mō-tel´), *v.* to threaten to verbally reveal forbidden activity. *"If you don't stop peein' in the pool, I **motel** Daddy!"*

moth·er (mə´-thər), *adj.* remaining or additional, particularly as possessed by or in relation to an individual. *"My oldest brother is all right, but **mother** brother's crazy."*

mud·dle (məd´-əl), *n. and v.* a prediction concerning sodden or soaked earth. *"Soak them pants, boy, or that **muddle** never come out."*

mul·let (məl´-ət), *v. and n.* to ponder a decision. *"Do I want a crew cut or a bowl cut? Hmmm. Lemme **mullet** over."*

mus·ket (məs´-kət), *v.* to declare a personal promise for future action. *"I **musket** my butt outta this bed and find a job . . . tomorrow."*

mys·ti·fy (mist´-əf-ī), *v. and conj.* a preamble to an excuse for having failed to hit or strike successfully. *"I wouldn't've **mystify** hadn't've been so drunk."*

Nn

na·ked (nā´-kəd), *n. and v.* a declaration of the capability of others. *"I'll do what I want, an' **naked** do what they want."*

MYSTIFY

NEEDLE

nap·kin (nap´-kən), *n. and v.* a negotiation presuming a doze; commonly used by children. *"If I take a napkin I go?"*

nav·i·gate (nav´-ə-gāt), *v. and n.* to lack possession of a closable, usually hinged barrier. *"I drove through the fence 'cause the dang fool did navigate."*

nee·dle (nēd´-əl), *v.* to desire urgently. *"After I finish this, I'm gonna needle little vacation."*

New Hamp·shire (nü-ham´-shər), *n. and adv.* a confident declaration concerning the edible parts of a fresh pig. *"That old leftover ham made everybody sick, but this New Hampshire does taste good."*

No·ah (nō´-ə), *v.* to have acquaintance or comprehension of. *"Anyone **Noah** guy with a boat we could use?"*

no·ti·fied (nōt´-əf-īd), *v. and conj.* to claim understanding, conditionally; often used as an excuse to cover ignorance. *"I woulda **notified** been told."*

nui·sance (nü´-sints), *adj. and adv.* pertaining to the duration of an object's existence. *"Old Tom's gun ain't been **nuisance** 1962."*

Oo

obliv·i·ate (ä-bliv´-ē-āt), *n. and v.* a declaration of a confident conviction concerning the history of another's mastication. *"**Obliviate** the whole thing."*

OBLIVIATE

OFFICIAL

ob·long (ä´-blȯng), *n. and v.* a statement concerning the speaker's feeling of being comfortably, or uncomfortably, located. *"I need to get back down south. This is not where **oblong**."*

odor (ō´-dər), *adj.* a comparative term describing the advanced existence of a thing or person. *"She's **odor** than dirt."*

od·ys·sey (ä´-də-sē), *v.* to suggest the duty or obligation of another to notice a particular thing. *"You **odyssey** the rack on her sister."*

of·fi·cial (ə-fish´-əl), *n. and v.* a prediction concerning the future of an aquatic craniate vertebrate. *"Everybody knows **official** taste better if you squeeze a little lemon on after you cook it."*

om·e·let (äm´-lət), *n. and v.* to allow another a thing or action. *"If you apologize, **omelet** you outta here alive."*

onus (ōn´-əs), *v. and n.* to be in the possession or control of other persons. *"We just work here. He don't **onus**."*

op·pose (əp´-ōz), *prep. and n.* into an elevated position on more than one thing. *"Let's climb **oppose** trees."*

oral (ȯr´-əl), *conj. and n.* an alternative scenario, usually promising an unpleasant action. *"Listen up, boy. You better clean your room good **oral** ground you for a week."*

OMELET

PARIS

out·line (aút´-līn), *adv. and v.* to be publicly relaying untruthful statements. *"My ex-husband been **outline** about what I did."*

pac·i·fy (pas´-əf-ī), *v. and conj.* during a contest, to overtake a competitor, under certain conditions. *"Dale Earnhardt was a fearless racer. He was like, 'I don't care what you do. I'll **pacify** feel like it.' "*

par·a·lyze (per-ə-līz´), *n.* two untruths. *"She said I was ugly and fat. That's a **paralyze**! Well, actually, it's one lie. I'm not fat!"*

Par·is (par´-əs), *n. and v.* used to express or describe the state of being of a set of two things. *"That salesman told me these French shoes were comfortable, but dang, this **Paris** killin' me."*

pas·ture (pas´-chŭr), *adv.* traveling by something owned or occupied by another. *"Hey, Charla, we're drivin' right **pasture** house."*

path·o·log·i·cal (path-ə-lä´-ji-kəl), *n. and adj.* a direction chosen upon reasoned reflection. *"We jus' took the **pathological** man would take."*

per·so·na (pərs-ōn´-ə), *n. and prep.* a reference to the location of a small strapped satchel usually carried by a woman. *"The cop said if you leave your **persona** table, you're just askin' for trouble."*

pe·so (pā´-sō), *v. and conj.* to provide legal tender in order to move on. *"Will you just **peso** we can leave?"*

PASTURE

PICKLE

pes·ter (pest´-ər), *n. and conj.* an annoying or irritating person, with the rhetorical implication of a nonexistent option. *"Is that kid a **pester** what?"*

pet·rol (pet´-rəl), *n. and v.* a domesticated animal performing the rehearsed behavior of turning over. *"Show me a trick. I wanna see your **petrol** over and play dead."*

phar·i·see (far´-ə-sē), *n. and v.* declaring visual cognition of a gathering for trade and entertainment. *"Every time I go to the **pharisee** somebody missin' a finger."*

pick·le (pik´-əl), *n. and v.* a prediction concerning a particular choice. *"Slick Rick knows horses real good, so I'm bettin' his **pickle** win."*

pic·ture (pik´-chŭr), *v.* to have pried loose using an appendage or tool. *"Right in front of the whole class you picture nose."*

pig·ment (pig´-mənt), *n. and v.* an emotional attribution of past feeling about a particular swine or heavyset person. *"Yeah, I'm cryin'! That pigment the world to me. You said we were havin' chicken!"*

pi·lot (pīl´-ət), *v. and n.* to place one thing on top of another. *"My wife was servin' mashed potatoes last night and I said, 'Pilot on, baby, pilot on!' "*

pim·ple (pimp´-əl), *n. and v.* a prediction regarding the future action of a purveyor of prostitution. *"Look, John, you're cute and all, but my pimple kill me if I don't charge you full fare."*

PICTURE

PIONEER

pi·o·neer (pī´-ən-ir), *n. and prep.* concerning the location of a crusted pastry. *"This place is called the Pie Hut, man. What do you mean you ain't got no **pioneer**?"*

pis·tol (pis´-til), *v. and conj.* to continue urination up to a certain moment. *"I drank forty-one beers and I think I could **pistol** the sun comes up."*

piz·za (pēts´-ə), *n. and v.* to make a declarative statement about any person named Peter. *"He loves wearing that dress, man. No doubt about it, that **pizza** weird guy."*

plane (plān´), *v.* being in the act of mischievous frolic. *"I will kill you! Trust me, I ain't **plane** around."*

plan·et (plan´-it), *v. and n.* to organize something in advance. *"Umm, Lieutenant Custer, the next time you decide to take on ten thousand Indians, you might wanna **planet** a little better."*

po·rous (pòr´-əs), *v. and n.* to dispense liquid for others. *"Hey, baby doll, could you **porous** another cup of coffee?"*

post·er (pōs´-tər), *adj. and prep.* acting according to a rule or agreed-upon behavior. *"We ain't **poster** leave until in the mornin'."*

prop·er (präp´-ər), *v. and n.* to lean a woman against an object for the purpose of counteracting gravitational pull. *"A real gentleman wouldn't just **proper** in the corner when she's had too much to drink."*

PLANET

PUMPKIN

pump·kin (pəmp´-kin), *n. and v.* a declaration about the capabilities of a device used for suctional or compressive transfer of liquid or air. *"No way that little **pumpkin** fill up these tires."*

punc·ture (pənk´-chŭr), *n. and adv.* a declaration concerning an obnoxious youth. *"That **puncture** had a smart mouth."*

Qq

quo·ta (kwōt´-ə), *v.* to relate, word for word, the statement of another. *"To **quota** great philosopher, it's spilt milk under the bridge."*

Rr

ran·som (ran´-səm), *v. and adj.* to have conducted certain operations or activities, such as a prescribed series of medical procedures for the purpose of discovering a problem or abnormality. *"I **ransom** tests and you're fine."*

rap·ture (rap´-chŭr), *n. and adv.* a declarative statement about a form of music combining spoken poetry and repetitive percussion. *"That **rapture** is playin' loud in that car."*

re·cede (rē´-sēd), *v.* to visually perceive a person or thing repeatedly. *"I seed him last Tuesday and then on Thursday I **recede** him."*

rec·ti·fy (rekt-əf-ī), *adj. and conj.* to suppose inebriation after continuing consumption. *"No thanks, barkeep. I'll be completely **rectify** have another drink."*

re·tard·ed (ri-tärd´-əd), *v. and prep.* to have withdrawn from employment at a particular moment in time. *"This here's the gold watch I got when I **retarded** age sixty-five."*

RECTIFY

RIGHTEOUS

righ·teous (rī´-chəs), *n. and adv.* a turn in the dextral direction. *"To get to Route 60 you go up this road about a mile, then make a **righteous** past the church."*

ru·mor (rüm´-ər), *n. and conj.* a phrase used in an ultimatum concerning personal space. *"Give me some **rumor** get outta my bed."*

Rus·sian (rəsh´-ən), *v.* acting in a hurried manner. *"Stop **Russian** around like a chicken with his head cut off."*

Ss

Sa·mo·an (sə-mō´-ən), *conj. and v.* involving a conclusion about the cutting or thrashing of plants with a bladed machine. *"I like workin' outside, **Samoan** my lawn ain't no big deal."*

sanc·tum (sank´-təm), *v. and n.* to have caused the submergence of more than one watercraft. *"He took two boats out fishin'. **Sanctum** both."*

Sat·ur·day (sat´-ər-dā), *adj. and n.* expressing sorrow about a particular twenty-four-hour period in a female's life. *"Her fiancé didn't show up. It's really **Saturday** got ruined like that."*

school (skül´), *v. and adj.* indicating one's sanguinity with a certain situation. *"Sure, man, if you wanna dance with my date, **school**."*

scoot·er (süt´-ər), *v. and adj.* to slide oneself in any direction while remaining seated, as done by a female. *"Tell your sister to **scooter** fat butt over so somebody else can sit down."*

SCHOOL

SEDATE

scur·vy (skər´-vē), *v. and adj.* being the opposite of straight. *"Check out Pam Anderson! Man, that body* ***scurvy**.*"

se·date (sid-āt´), *v. and n.* to have stated a time four hours before noon or midnight. *"You told me to come at nine o'clock, but Terry* ***sedate**.*"

sed·i·ment (sed´-ə-mənt), *v.* having stated something about one's intentions or opinions. *"I know what I said, and I know what I meant, but that is not what I* ***sediment**.*"

se·nior (sēn-yȯr´), *v. and adj.* to have visually perceived something belonging to another. *"Half the town* ***senior** wife with the gardener.*"

shad·ed (shād´-əd), *n. and v.* used to state that something greatly displeased or was despised by a female. *"My wife tried sushi and **shaded** it."*

sheep·herd·er (shē´-pər-dər), *n. and v.* having placed and released an object, as done by a female. *"I can't find 'em now, but I know **sheepherder** shoes right over here."*

sher·iff (sher´-əf), *v. and conj.* to offer a portion of, under certain conditions. *"All right, you don't have to **sheriff** you don't wanna."*

Sin·ga·pore (sing´-ə-pȯr), *v. and n.* to express oneself in song with exuberance. *"When I **Singapore** my heart into it."*

SHADED

SIREN

si·ren (sī´-rən), *conj. and v.* giving a reason for propelling oneself forward speedily, with a bounding stride. *"That crazy dude came at me with a hammer, **siren** as fast as I could . . . but I guess not fast enough."*

sit·u·ate (si´-chəw-āt), *conj. and v.* a phrase used to explain the consequences of someone else having consumed orally what belonged to the explainer. *"You don't get another piece of pie **situate** mine."*

skil·let (skil´-ət), *n.* acumen for a particular activity. *"I think it's safe to say, son, that you don't have the **skillet** takes to fry eggs."*

sluice (slüs´), *v. and adj.* to declare that a person or thing has escaped. *"My pet python **sluice**!"*

snow·man (snō´-man), *v. and adv.* to answer in the negative, emphatically. *"If you're askin' did I do it, the answer snowman."*

so·cial (sō´-shəl), *conj. and v.* an explanation re-garding actions taken to achieve a desired result from a specific female. *"I just gave that doggie some food social stop yappin' at me."*

so·da (sō´-də), *adv. and v.* an action or way of being including others. *"I like beer and soda my friends."*

sol·dier (sōl´-jūr), *v. and adj.* to have exchanged a person or object belonging to another for money. *"I hope you don't mind, dude, but I soldier mother on eBay."*

SOLDIER

SUMMER

starch (stärch´), *v. and adj.* to order a person or persons to turn on their motor or motors. *"Gentlemen, starch engines."*

sti·let·to (stə´-let-ō), *adv. and v.* to continue to allow an action of something or someone elderly. *"Sure she's sixty-two, but I stiletto lady Thompson climb in my bed once in a while."*

sum·ma·rize (sə´-mər-īz), *n. and v.* to intend or guarantee the fulfillment of an action to be pursued during the months following the June solstice and before the autumnal equinox. *"I almost drowned last August, so this summarize gonna learn to swim."*

sum·mer (səm´-ər), *n. and v.* the existence or condition of a subset or part of a group. *"Don't take it personal, Mrs. Herman. Summer cute and summer just plain ugly."*

sur·re·al (sər-rē´-əl), *n. and adv.* used to formally express enthusiasm to a superior. *"Yessir, Sergeant, I'm doin' good, **surreal** good."*

sur·round (sə-raúnd´), *v. and adv.* used to declare that something is or has been in the general vicinity. *"We done picked up the scent, so I know it **surround** here someplace."*

su·shi (sü´-shē), *n. and pron.* concerning the actions or response of a female in regard to one named Susan. *"We were gonna get married, but after I told her about **sushi** changed her mind."*

su·ture (sü´-chər), *v. and n.* to invite another to do as he or she pleases. *"He said he didn't want no anesthetic, and I said **suture** self."*

SUTURE

TABOO

syn·drome (sin´-drōm), *v. and n.* to dispatch a female to her place of residence. *"If we're at a bar and the wife gets drunk, I just syndrome."*

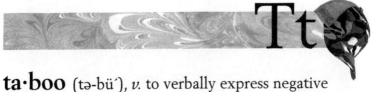

ta·boo (tə-bü´), *v.* to verbally express negative opinions about another or others. *"It ain't right for them folks taboo little Billy like that."*

tap·es·try (tap´-əs-trē), *v. and n.* to create a canal or opening for the purpose of drainage in a particular woody arborescent perennial. *"You might find some syrup if you tapestry."*

tar·na·tion (tär´-nā-shən), *adj. and n.* the complete and total population of a sovereign territorial state. *"The whole country is into NASCAR now. I'm talkin' 'bout the tarnation."*

Tau·rus (tȯr´-əs), *v. and adj.* to rend or split something belonging to a male. *"When he tried to pick up that penny, he **Taurus** underwear."*

taw·dry (tȯ´-drē), *prep. and n.* conveying toward or giving something to any person or creature with the name Audrey. *"If you think the dress is that ugly, why don't you give it **tawdry**? She's half blind, so she'll never know the difference."*

teat (tēt´), *v.* to consume and swallow a solid substance through the mouth. *"Mama, I didn't get enough **teat**."*

tele·cast (tel-i-kast´), *conj. and n.* regarding advice given to wait on any action so that it is not done before the deployment of a plaster mold used to ensure the immobility of a limb. *"Don't move your arm **telecast** gets put on it."*

TELECAST

TESTAMENT

ter·rain (tə-rān´), *prep. and n.* indicating a change bringing the descent of water droplets from a mass of condensed vapor. *"Those clouds could turn **terrain** any second, and this road'll turn to mud."*

ter·ror (ter´-ər), *v. and adj.* to rend or shred something from a woman, usually objects of adornment. *"I couldn't wait to get my wife back to the honeymoon suite so I could **terror** clothes off."*

tes·ta·ment (test´-ə-mənt), *n. and v.* a specific examination, indicated by the speaker's intention. *"When I told you I hope you pass the test, Darlene, that weren't the **testament**."*

tick·le (tik´-əl), *n. and v.* a prediction about the actions of a bloodsucking arachnid. *"If you don't use tweezers, that **tickle** be hard to get out."*

tie-dyed (tī´-dīd), *n. and v.* the expiration of a person named Tyler. *"Ty liked to sleep on the train tracks. Then **tie-dyed**."*

tight (tī´-ət), *v.* to unite or fasten a string, cord, or rope, usually in a knot or bow. *"If you don't want your shoe to come off, you can't go and leave the lace undone like that, son. You've got to **tight**. And when you **tight**, you got to **tight** real tight."*

tile (tī´-əl), *n. and v.* to predict the results of adorning oneself with a fashion accessory worn about the neck. *"Heck, Bubba, this here **tile** get you into any fancy restaurant you want."*

tippy (tip´-ē), *n.* extra money or gratuity paid in exchange for good service, as performed by a male. *"You don't give that waiter a **tippy** goes crazy."*

TIE-DYED

TIRE

tire (tī´-ər), *v. and n.* to restrain a female, as with ribbon, rope, or bungee cord. *"I thought I told you to **tire** down!"*

tor·toise (tòrt´-əs), *v. and n.* to have imparted knowledge or wisdom to a group. *"That stupid teacher never **tortoise** nothin'."*

trac·tor (trakt´-ər), *v. and n.* having traced, hunted, and found a female. *"She ran, but the police **tractor** down."*

tur·bine (tər´-bīn), *n. and v.* regarding reaction to a monetary exchange by a female. *"Just 'cause she's a pretty lady, I got no objection **turbine** the next round."*

Uu

uni·sex (yü´-nə-seks), *n. and adj.* a phrase used
to connect another with any device or item employed
for sensual pleasure. *"Just me, **unisex** toy is my idea of a
party."*

urine (yər´-ən), *n. and v.* a statement declaring the
predicament of another. *"I hate to say it, but if you need
to go potty, bud, **urine** big trouble."*

Vv

van·i·ty (van´-ət-ē), *n. and pron.* indicating past
possession by a male of a cargo-carrying vehicle. *"His
new van is way nicer than that other **vanity** had."*

ver·ti·go (vər´-ti-gō), *prep. and v.* a conditional negotiation concerning the further movement of a speci-
fied female. *"**Vertigo** to the dance I wanna know that
she'll be home by midnight."*

URINE

WATER

Ww

wa·fer (wā´-fər), *v. and prep.* to request another person to cease their forward motion. *"Hey, **wafer** me."*

wag·on (wag´-ən), *v.* whipping back and forth. *"That dog just bit me in the face, then sat there **wagon** his tail."*

wal·let (wäl´-ət), *conj. and n.* indicating temporal or contradictory conditions. *"**Wallet** appears that I stole your wallet, I didn't."*

wa·ter (wät´-ər), *n. and v.* used to introduce an inquiry concerning the future. *"I just wanna know, **water** my options?"*

wa·ter·front (wät-ər-frənt´), *pron. and n.* used to inquire about the unseen forward-looking side of a female. *"From the back she looks great, but before I ask her out I wanna know **waterfront** looks like."*

wed·ding (we´-din), *v.* making saturated with liquid. *"They been married for seventy years, and now he goes and celebrates by **wedding** his pants."*

Wednes·day (wenz´-dā), *adv. and n.* introducing an inquiry about the future date of an event. *"**Wednesday** we're supposed to get married? 'Cause I might be busy."*

whit·ey (wī´-tē), *adv. and n.* introducing an inquiry about the intention of a male's action. *"Aww, **whitey** have to go and do that for?"*

WHITEY

WIRE

wil·low (wil-ō´), *v. and adj.* introducing an inquiry about the future or future actions of an elderly person. *"I wonder **willow** George Bush do somethin' about the economy?"*

win·dows (win´-dōz), *adv.* indicating the future action of a group. *"Hey, Carl, tell me **windows** dogs come back."*

wire (wī´-ər), *adv. and n.* introducing an inquiry as to the motivation of or reason for an action. *"So, uh, **wire** you here?"*

wood·en (wŭ´-dən), *v.* to have fervent desire for an event not to occur. *"I can tell you I **wooden** want her as my wife."*

wor·ry (wər´-ē), *adv. and n.* regarding the location of a male. *"No, I don't got no idea **worry** went."*

wres·tle (res´-əl), *n. and v.* indicating or predicting the future effects of a period of inactivity. *"A full night's **wrestle** do you good."*

Yy

yacht (yät´), *n. and v.* to advise or urge someone toward making a wise choice. *"**Yacht** to put out that cigarette while you're pumpin' gas."*

Yale (yāl´), *v.* to emit vocal tones at a high volume. *"I heard you the first time. You don't have to **Yale**."*

WORRY

ZANY

yawn (yȯn´), *n. and prep.* indicating the position of another. *"Watch where you're steppin'!* **Yawn** *my foot!"*

Yid·dish (yi-dish´), *n.* a vessel designed for the holding and carrying of food; specifically, such an object of a particular person. *"Where are your manners?! Take* **Yiddish** *to the kitchen when you're finished!"*

Yu·ca·tán (yü-kə-tan´), *n. and v.* allowing for the ability of another person to expose their epidermis to the sun's rays for a period of time, causing it to darken in hue. *"It's your choice:* **Yucatán** *in a booth or* **Yucatán** *at the beach."*

Zz

za·ny (zā´-nē), *v. and n.* indicating another's proclamations. *"This guy was standin' right here the whole time, and now he's* **zany** *didn't see nothin'."*

ABOUT THE AUTHOR

JEFF FOXWORTHY is the largest-selling comedy-recording artist in history, a multiple Grammy Award nominee, and the bestselling author of thirteen books. He stars in and executive produces the television series *Blue Collar TV,* based on *Blue Collar Comedy Tour, The Movie,* which first aired on Comedy Central and became the highest-rated movie in the channel's history. The sequel, *Blue Collar Comedy Tour, Rides Again,* has exceeded 2.6 million in DVD sales and in March 2006, the Blue Collar boys will reunite to shoot *Blue Collar Comedy Tour, One for the Road* at the Warner Theatre in Washington, D.C. Jeff also has an HBO special and two Showtime specials to his credit. His syndicated weekly radio show, *The Foxworthy Countdown,* is carried in more than 220 markets across the United States.

Offstage and -screen, Jeff has helped the Duke University Children's Hospital raise over $4 million in the last four years and is Honorary Chairman of the Duke Children's Classic Golf Tournament. A Georgia native, he lives with his wife and two daughters in Atlanta.